Ylonia Berger and Mira Brahe

Economastrologics
A Stock Market Zodiac

Illustrations by

Elvy

Very Important Press

First edition, 2025

Grateful acknowledgment is made to Janderson Gomes for permission to use the LaTeX e-book template Caraumã. Template copyright © 2024 by Janderson Gomes. All rights reserved.

ISBN: 979-8-9909233-3-1

Published by Very Important Press

PREFACE

FOR THOUSANDS OF YEARS, when faced with the question of fate, which is ultimately the question *why*, humanity has looked to the stars. For presumably just as long, when faced with the question of money, which is primarily the question of *how*, humanity has looked, with laudable creativity but a remarkably universal preference for ease[1] to the world around us. And for probably as long as humanity has existed, when faced with the question of men[2], which is often the question of *what the fuck*, humanity must search even further afield.

It is the confluence of all of these questions, the central overlap in the tripartite Venn diagram, to which we turn today.

There is a meme whose popularity transcends platforms, which has been riffed upon in blogs, posts, tweets, skeets, vines (RIP), and even in real world conversations. Present-day artists stitch their interpretations onto pillows and print their designs on shirts. Future historians will

---

[1] Whomst amongst us would not prefer to find a winning lottery ticket between the couch cushions to a life of grueling farm work, or worse, an 8-hour day in a comfortable office clicking at screens?

[2] We hear the squawking already: "not all men!" Don't be so hysterical, honey. If you are a man who does not provoke the question of *what the fuck,* you probably know already that the joke does not apply to you. The authors are aware from third-, second-, and regrettably first-hand experience that gullibility, greed, and lack of critical thinking are gender neutral traits. Alternately, we could, with sardonic glee, reach for the same fig leaf as our pre-twenty-first-century academic predecessors, and claim that we use use "men" to mean simply "humanity." We decline to do so, because those academic predecessors were so often insufferable pricks, and we would prefer to remain sufferable. For now.

write treatises and theses about what it implies about early 21st century culture. Our descendants will upload it to their neurosocialfeeds over a sepia-toned image of Abraham Lincoln, captioning it "ancient online proverb."

While it has been posted over many images, the meme reads:

"Economics is just astrology for men."

We have studied economics, the dismal science, with great diligence[3] and great bemusement[4], astrology with equal parts skepticism[5] and laziness[6], and men with fond[7] exasperation. We have found the meme to be entirely true, but due to a lack of an appropriate scientific framework[8], it is one of those fictions that is truer than reality.

Finding ourselves with an excess of time and no reason *not* to be silly, we have followed in the proud tradition of men, and gifted to the world something that was neither wanted, nor needed, nor useful. We have taken the meme not only literally, but to its absurdest conclusion, for this stock market zodiac.

We can foresee some distress at our derision. Some may contend that economics is justified by mathematics, whereas astrology is mere vibes. Others may contend that astrology is based on stars and planets, which are generally agreed to be real, and economics is just made up numbers. The gendered tone of each protestation is left to the reader, whom we trust to provide it with depressing consistency.

Our answer is: economists and astrologers often sound awfully similar, and similarly awful, especially when it comes to pomposity. It is equalizing, even efficient, to parody them simultaneously.

---

[3]One of us.

[4]The other.

[5]Both of us.

[6]Ibid.

[7]Mostly, anyway.

[8]Can you believe that this was written with a straight face? We can't, either.

Thesis and antithesis, brought together in an environment of extreme boredom, have been alchemized into this gloriously self-important synthesis.

In other words, this is all bullshit. But we had fun with it, and we hope you do as well.

The authors would like to acknowledge the reality that most people are probably skimming past the overwrought prose to get to the pretty pictures, and while we find this eminently understandable, we would rather not face the legal or karmic consequences of an overhasty reader missing something quite important. We reiterate our disclaimers, this time in **boldface, so you notice: This book is a work of parody.** Even more so than any other text about either economics or astrology, this book is **for entertainment purposes only.** Under no circumstances should this text be construed as financial, legal, medical, religious, personal, interpersonal, or any other kind of advice. If you *really* want to use this for advice, no you don't; but if you do so anyway, please tell us how it works out for you. We love schadenfreude.

Even more than we love schadenfreude, we genuinely love the people who helped with this work. The authors would like to thank Elvy for the wonderful illustrations. We marvel at their creativity in visualizing such absurd abstractions. They brought our silly joke zodiac to life, and they did so as art is meant to be made: not with AI, but with their own blood, sweat, and swearing.[9] We thank them also for not telling us to fuck off with this nonsense.

Additionally, we would like to thank the Group Chat With Many Names for making the work day go faster. Thank you to some men in particular for your assistance (you know what you did), and men in general, for the inspiration. You know what you did.

---

[9] In fact, no part of this work was created with AI. You can tell, because no mere machine could produce such a ridiculous, febrile, overwritten text as the brains of the authors when sufficiently bored. We refrain from threatening a lawsuit for copyright infringement if you use this work to train a LLM, because we are not a large publisher with an army of lawyers, but if you do feed this to an AI: fuck you. We hope you step on a Lego.

Contents

Preface   iii

How to Use This Book   1

The Signs   3

    Calls   5

    Dividends   6

    Leverage   7

    Futures   8

    Volatility   9

    Crypto   10

    Puts   11

    Charts   12

    Interest Rates   13

    Earnings   14

    Bonds   15

    Equities   16

Risings   17

    Death Cross   18

    Iron Condor   19

    Butterfly   20

    Hindenburg   21

    Momentum   22

Double Top 23

Spread 24

Long Straddle 25

Short Strangle 26

Fibonacci 27

Bull 28

Bear 29

Conclusion   31

About the Authors   35

I
How to Use This Book

E CONOMASTROLOGICS stems from the realization that from natal charts to the NASDAQ, from retrograde to RSI, from celestial balance to account balances, it's all just a bunch of little lines going up and down.

For thousands of years, humans have used historical patterns in the stars to guarantee future results; for hundreds of years, we have extrapolated this to the markets. Our economically-minded ancestors have already given us such remarkable strategies as moon phase trading.[1] Neither of these strategies has a stellar record, but they provide an ideal foundation for the core insight of Economastrologics.

This new framework brings together the explanatory power of economics and astrology, with the confidence of a mediocre man. In other words, we provide to the world a means of provoking the questions of *why, how,* and certainly *what the fuck* all at once, and we preen with self-satisfaction to do so.

Now, let us move on to the mechanisms of Economastrologics.

---

[1] We must follow a brief tangent, and offer an apology to moon phase traders placing their trades from the International Space Station. As you are located closer to the moon, sun, *and* stars, you should be ideally placed to benefit from Economastrologics, but your spatial advantage is offset by the spacial disadvantage created by your rapid orbit around the Earth. Your moon phases are too short for them to have any causal effect on the markets. We apologize for any inconvenience.

Whether you are more familiar with birth charts or candlestick charts, you are in luck: Economastrologics needs neither. If you know the date, time, and place of your birth, you could draw some lines on the zodiac to chart your sign and rising sign. Voila, this tells you who you are as a person and determines your trading strategy![2] When[3] you lock in your guaranteed[4] profits, we told you so!

If you know the jargon for your trading strategy, simply seek out your sign and rising sign from the list. Voila! This tells you who you are as a person and determines your fate![5] Perhaps this validates your life choices. Perhaps it offers guidance on what you should be doing differently in your life. Whether it is vindication by vibes or celestial constructive criticism, we told you so![6]

Now that you know how to interpret Economastrologics, you can start implementing its explanatory power into your life. This is a simple process of speaking confidently, disregarding contrary evidence, and using as much jargon as possible, in order to make your listener stop questioning your sanity and begin questioning their own.[7]

As you can see from your present feelings of confusion, annoyance, and secondhand mortification, Economastrologics is a powerful and effective rhetorical tool. We trust you will find it as relevant and empowering in your life as it is in ours. You can thank us later.

---

[2] Let us reiterate: holy shit, this is not financial advice. Please don't do this.

[3] If. Please, if.

[4] This is stressing us out to write.

[5] It really doesn't.

[6] The astute reader will note that we have developed a framework where no matter what conclusions you draw, we are taking credit for being right. This is, of course, by design, and in the best—or at least, most common—tradition of economists and astrologers alike.

[7] We find this particularly effective when making excuses, e.g., "my trade totally would have made money, except the moon is in Death Cross," "sorry, but I can't date a Dividends," "I'll pay you back once Hindenburg is in retrograde," and similar.

II
THE SIGNS

JUST AS ASTROLOGY arranges the sky into twelve sectors through which the sun passes each year, Economastrologics has twelve star signs. These are determined by your birth date, or trading strategy, as you prefer. Each sign is associated with one of the elements[1] and has both positive and negative traits.

Fire signs are bold risk takers. They are confident in their abilities and can back it up, but sometimes they're only looking out for themselves. The fire signs are Volatility, Futures, and Leverage.

Water signs are quiet and reserved. It's no shock that they know their stuff, but that would require cracking open these tough nuts. They may have a reputation for miserliness, but with their friends, they are generous and beloved. The water signs are Bonds, Interest Rates, and Dividends.

Air signs have the confidence of a fire sign, but all of it is false. They are bold and outlandish, usually with completely intolerable bro energy, but that arrogance is just a facade over a sweet heart and intelligent mind. The air signs are Puts, Crypto, and Charts.

Earth signs are secretly a little spicy! You wouldn't guess it from the calm, respectable way they present themselves, but watch out, they are bound to surprise you. The earth signs are Calls, Earnings, and Equities.

---

[1]Not from the periodic table. We didn't go that far.

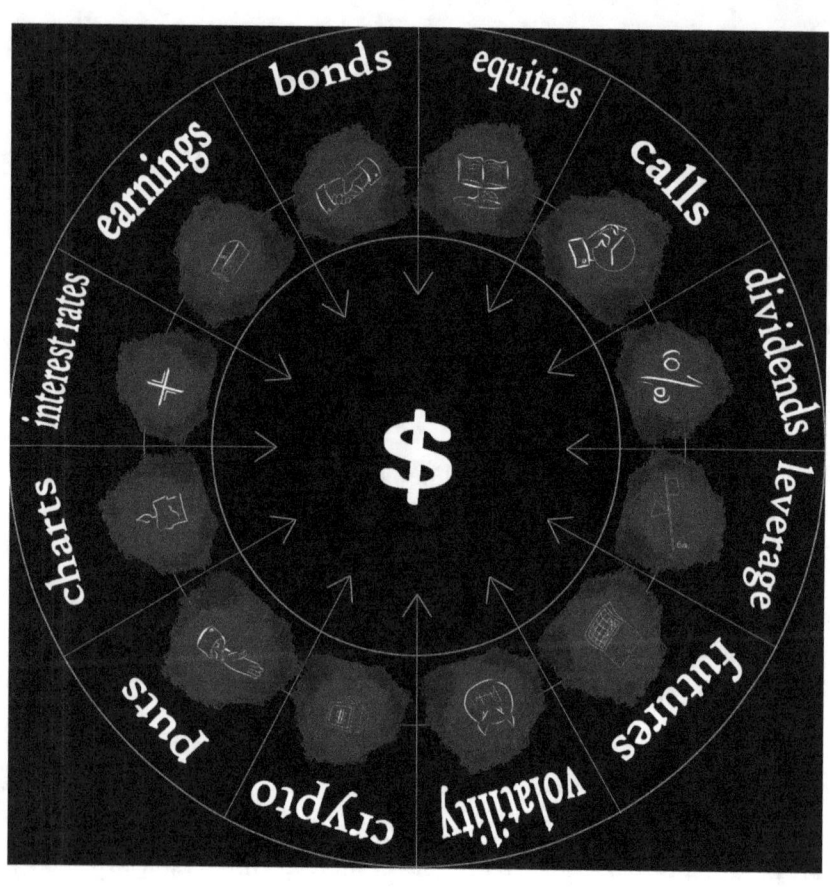

II.1 CALLS

CALLS: The constant optimist of your friend group, you light up a room and are the life of the party. People just seem to get you, and you love to be the center of attention. All that energy has an expiration date, though, and if you don't take care of yourself, you might get burned.

    Dates: March 21-April 19
    Element: Water
    Personality Traits: Ambitious, Disciplined, Responsible
    Love Match: Puts, Equities
    Other Half/Soulmate: Bonds
    At Odds With: Dividends, but only once a quarter

II.2   DIVIDENDS

DIVIDENDS: The picture of reliability. You share your prosperity, and you'll always support the people around you. You like to spice it up every few months, but even if you have your own highs and lows, you'll still be there. Some people might take you for granted, but your true friends cherish you for life.

Dates: April 20-May 20
Element: Earth
Personality Traits: Resourceful, Determined, Passionate
Love Match: Equities, Puts
Other Half/Soulmate: Equities
At Odds With: Calls, but only once a quarter

II.3 LEVERAGE

L EVERAGE: Everything in your life you do to the extreme. You have a great sense of humor, but you've got no patience for those who can't keep up. You're an adrenaline junkie and love to experience the highest highs, even if you know that a small change could cause insurmountable problems...but, hey, that's an "if" problem.

Dates: May 21-June 20

Element: Fire

Personality Traits: Optimistic, Thrill Seeker, Passionate

Love Match: Volatility

Other Half/Soulmate: Futures

At Odds With: Charts, they love you – but you can't find it in your-self to reciprocate

II.4   FUTURES

FUTURES: You're the mom friend who has their life together. You aren't afraid to put yourself into extremely risky situations, because you know how to bail yourself out if you need to. Be careful not to get cocky, though: when things go wrong, they go *really* wrong, and you have a tendency to spiral. You're adored by all, but very picky with who you entertain in real relationships.

Dates: June 21-July 20
Element: Fire
Personality Traits: Confident, Charismatic, Generous
Love Match: Crypto
Other Half/Soulmate: Equities
At Odds With: Dividends

II.5 VOLATILITY

VOLATILITY: While you have certain predictable tendencies, the extent to which you do anything is far from certain. You're the friend that isn't afraid to take big swings regardless of the outcome and who might get impacted–after all, that's how you get results.

Dates: July 23-August 22

Element: Fire

Personality Traits: Determined, Energetic, Honest

Love Match: Leverage – lots of passion, but long term will result in mutually assured destruction

Other Half/Soulmate: Charts, but you're the one being chased

At Odds With: Bonds

II.6 CRYPTO

CRYPTO: It's complicated, and that's not a bad thing. You've got big dreams, and you don't sweat the details, even though sometimes maybe you should. You're easily infatuated by the latest fad, so think twice before committing—once you make up your mind, you're a ride or die. You'll go down with your ship and die on the mountains you make out of molehills.

Dates: August 23-September 22
Element: Air
Personality Traits: Innovative, Independent
Love Match: Futures
Other Half/Soulmate: Leverage
At Odds With: Bonds

II.7 PUTS

PUTS: You're a bit of a pessimist, even though you insist you're just a realist. You're creative, and you've always got a way to turn a worst-case scenario to your advantage. You're a little abrasive at first, but that's just to keep the riffraff out—once someone falls for you, they're yours for life.

Dates: September 23-October 22
Element: Air
Personality Traits: Curious, Good Communicator, Adaptable
Love Match: Calls
Other Half/Soulmate: Leverage
At Odds With: Interest Rates

II.8 CHARTS

CHARTS: You're the vibes friend. Things can change for you in the spur of the moment and suddenly you're on a completely different path. You can recognize patterns in your past behavior – whether you choose to actually pay attention to the outcome and change it is up for debate.

Dates: October 23-November 21

Element: Air

Personality Traits: Charming, Diplomatic, Social Butterfly

Love Match: Leverage, Crypto

Other Half/Soulmate: Vol, but you're always going to be the one chasing

At Odds With: Interest Rates, Earnings

II.9 INTEREST RATES

INTEREST RATES: You're deliberate—someone should be, in this economy! You know what you want, and you'll make your situation work to get you there. However, you never do anything halfway, and if things go wrong for you, you'll make sure everyone hears about it.

Dates: November 22-December 21

Element: Water

Personality Traits: Empathetic, Compassionate, Wise

Love Match: Calls

Other Half/Soulmate: Bonds

At Odds With: Charts, Crypto

II.10 EARNINGS

EARNINGS: An ambivert through and through. You're either a complete homebody in your favorite, worn through PJs or you're closing down the clubs. You're a natural leader and everyone wants to be your friend, even if you'd sometimes rather do your own thing instead of having to give guidance all the time.

Dates: December 22-January 19
Element: Earth
Personality Traits: Analytical, Hardworking, Loyal
Love Match: Puts, Calls
Other Half/Soulmate: Vol
At Odds With: Charts

II.11 BONDS

BONDS: You're a planner, always looking for what comes next, even if that means you're never truly rooted in the moment. You've got a 10-year plan, but what about the next 5 minutes? You crave consistency in all aspects of your life. Others turn to you when they need your sense of security.

Dates: January 20-February 18

Element: Water

Personality Traits: Intuitive, Protective, Loyal, Persuasive

Love Match: Interest Rates

Other Half/Soulmate: Calls

At Odds With: Vol—you've had occasional flings, and it always ends in tears

II.12 EQUITIES

EQUITIES: You love variety in your life and can't be pinned down! Your interests are varied, you can be friends with everyone, and everyone usually finds something to like about you. You can cause some unexpected ripples when you have personal down days, but year over year, you keep progressing and growing.

Dates: February 19-March 20
Element: Earth
Personality Traits: Pragmatic, Patient
Love Match: Calls
Other Half/Soulmate: Dividends
At Odds With: Volatility, Crypto

III

Risings

RELIABLE SOURCES have informed us that while your star sign determines much of your personality, your moon sign, or rising, is arguably more important. We have forgotten the reason for this.

According to astrological tradition, your rising sign is determined by the placement of the moon at the time of your birth. If you happen to know the time when you were born, congratulations, but as to how this correlates to a particular sign, we have no idea. Nonetheless, in the mode of economists, astrologers, and men everywhere, a lack of knowledge does not stop us from opining; see the chart at the end of the chapter.

Another way of ascertaining your Economastrologics rising sign is through the economist's traditional divination method, which is known as technical analysis. Just as lines can be drawn between stars to form constellations, so do the studies on a chart form a picture.

The method is simple. Choose a security associated with your star sign, overlay it with various studies, and notice the picture created by the confluence of the studies. This picture is your rising sign, and according to many economists, should determine your trading strategy.

If you are unfamiliar with technical analysis in general or which studies to choose for your chart, we recommend finding the nearest available man, and asking him to explain. Now that you have a few minutes of peace while he manfully drones on, you can simply read the rising signs and pick the one that you like best.

III.1   DEATH CROSS

DEATH CROSS: You're a worrier, but that's only because you care. Even when things are good, you tend to dwell on the past, and sometimes you fret that your best days may be behind you. Don't let the past overshadow the future, and remember to enjoy the here and now.

III.2   IRON CONDOR

IRON CONDOR: You're happy when the people around you are happy. You always leave some room for grace, but you have standards. You're great at setting boundaries, but reciprocity is important to you—if someone oversteps, you'll give them instant karma.

III.3 Butterfly

BUTTERFLY: You're a perfectionist, and proud of it. You are happiest when everything is in its proper place, but that doesn't mean everything has to be the same. You shine when different things work together in harmony, but sometimes get sulky when things are disordered.

III.4 HINDENBURG

HINDENBURG: Harbinger of doom, anyone? You're always thinking about the worst case scenario and you expect disaster to strike at any time. You know that a healthy dose of cynicism just means you're prepared for that one-in-a-million moment. If it happens, you'll have the solution; if not, it's a pleasant surprise. You win, either way.

III.5 MOMENTUM

M OMENTUM: When you're up, you're up, and when you're down, you're down. Either way, you're committed. You are a bit hardheaded and set in your ways regardless of extenuating circumstances. When you're determined, stuff is getting done, but far be it from anyone to try to stop you or get in your way.

III.6 Double Top

D OUBLE TOP: Very into power dynamics, you aren't afraid to assert your dominance. People look to you for your decision making and trust you to lead them in the right direction. Be mindful of that responsibility, though, because if you let your competitive side get the best of you, it's not just you at risk.

III.7   SPREAD

SPREAD: You're pragmatic and easy to get along with for most people. You have an opinion on everything, but you always look for different perspectives and try to see others' side of the story before making any decisions. This does limit you sometimes, but better safe than sorry.

III.8   LONG STRADDLE

LONG STRADDLE: If the taste of champagne could be a person, it would be you. You aren't afraid to throw money around as long as something is moving and shaking! You can't be tied down, but you tend to get bored easily, so you can be flighty at times. You'll thrive with someone to ground you (and maybe is better with the money management).

III.9   SHORT STRANGLE

SHORT STRANGLE: You have your comfort zone, and you're staying in it, thank you very much. You're fine riding the line between peace and disaster, because you know your limits and your boundaries are impeccable. Just be careful not to feign ignorance in the face of change—you don't do well with chaos.

III.10 FIBONACCI

FIBONACCI: You subscribe to an academic view of the world. Everything has its reasons and everything can be explained rationally. You likely think this whole economic astrology is made up and couldn't possibly actually identify personality traits. You may feel a little called out now, but admit it, this was more accurate than you thought it would be.

III.11 BULL

BULL: You radiate confidence in everything you do. You have high expectations for yourself and others, but you're always encouraging. You don't necessarily get bogged down if things don't work out in the short run, because you know everything happens for a reason, even if you don't know what it is at the time. Everything will work out in the long run.

III.12   BEAR

BEAR: You're a thinker and a bit of a cynic. You understand that everything ebbs and flows, and you're not afraid to benefit from the downturns. You always speak your mind, and you never walk on eggshells. That makes you unpopular sometimes, but that's fine—you're out to win. People take awhile to accept you, and you have a hard time warming up to others, but your candor brings them around in the end.

Birthday	3/21-4/19	4/20-5/20	5/21-6/20	6/21-7/20	7/23-8/22	8/23-9/22
Sign	Calls	Dividends	Leverage	Futures	Volatility	Crypto
12:00am-2:00am	Bear	Long Straddle	Spread	Iron Condor	Fibonacci	Butterfly
2:00am-4:00am	Bull	Bear	Long Straddle	Spread	Iron Condor	Fibonacci
4:00am-6:00am	Death Cross	Bull	Bear	Long Straddle	Spread	Iron Condor
6:00am-8:00am	Double Top	Death Cross	Bull	Bear	Long Straddle	Spread
8:00am-10:00am	Hindenburg	Double Top	Death Cross	Bull	Bear	Long Straddle
10:00am-12:00pm	Momentum	Hindenburg	Double Top	Death Cross	Bull	Bear
12:00pm-2:00pm	Short Strangle	Momentum	Hindenburg	Double Top	Death Cross	Bull
2:00pm-4:00pm	Butterfly	Short Strangle	Momentum	Hindenburg	Double Top	Death Cross
4:00pm-6:00pm	Fibonacci	Butterfly	Short Strangle	Momentum	Hindenburg	Double Top
6:00pm-8:00pm	Iron Condor	Fibonacci	Butterfly	Short Strangle	Momentum	Hindenburg
8:00pm-10:00pm	Spread	Iron Condor	Fibonacci	Butterfly	Short Strangle	Momentum
10:00pm-12:00am	Long Straddle	Spread	Iron Condor	Fibonacci	Butterfly	Short Strangle

Birthday	9/23-10/22	10/23-11/22	11/23-12/21	12/22-1/19	1/20-2/18	2/19-3/19
Sign	Puts	Charts	Interest Rates	Earnings	Bonds	Equities
12:00am-2:00am	Short Strangle	Momentum	Hindenburg	Double Top	Death Cross	Bull
2:00am-4:00am	Butterfly	Short Strangle	Momentum	Hindenburg	Double Top	Death Cross
4:00am-6:00am	Fibonacci	Butterfly	Short Strangle	Momentum	Hindenburg	Double Top
6:00am-8:00am	Iron Condor	Fibonacci	Butterfly	Short Strangle	Momentum	Hindenburg
8:00am-10:00am	Spread	Iron Condor	Fibonacci	Butterfly	Short Strangle	Momentum
10:00am-12:00pm	Long Straddle	Spread	Iron Condor	Fibonacci	Butterfly	Short Strangle
12:00pm-2:00pm	Bear	Long Straddle	Spread	Iron Condor	Fibonacci	Butterfly
2:00pm-4:00pm	Bull	Bear	Long Straddle	Spread	Iron Condor	Fibonacci
4:00pm-6:00pm	Death Cross	Bull	Bear	Long Straddle	Spread	Iron Condor
6:00pm-8:00pm	Double Top	Death Cross	Bull	Bear	Long Straddle	Spread
8:00pm-10:00pm	Hindenburg	Double Top	Death Cross	Bull	Bear	Long Straddle
10:00pm-12:00am	Momentum	Hindenburg	Double Top	Death Cross	Bull	Bear

IV

CONCLUSION

While we are aware that absolutely no one asked for this, we trust you are now supremely delighted to have encountered it. We hope—no, we *know*—that your new knowledge of Economastrologics has empowered you. We may even be so bold as to say that it has changed the course of your life. We answer your unspoken words with all the obnoxiousness of the smarmiest man you have ever had the misfortune to meet: you're welcome.[1]

We now brave a trial that may be unfamiliar to many of the individuals we have so often disparaged in this book: we do not jump to conclusions, but saunter slowly, taking a detour towards reflection.

As has been reiterated several times throughout this book, Economastrologics is a farce that arose from the authors' riffs on a meme. Nonetheless, during the process of writing jokes and assigning signs to various friends[2], we were forced to experiment with things such as "research," which led us to "thoughtfulness," and worst of all, "introspection." Le gasp! Quelle horreur!

The reader will forgive us[3], then, for a brief moment of earnestness.

---

[1]Let us assure you, that felt as gross to write as it surely does to read. Sorry. (...no. We're really not.)

[2]And no, we aren't saying what signs were based on whom. If you know, you know.

[3]We hope. If you found this entire book unforgivable, we despair of you, but we can't say you're *wrong*.

We did more reading than we initially intended.[4] We found that astrology actually is deeply entwined with mythology and archetypes, and though we still don't believe that your birthday determines anything about you, we do believe that men's[5] choices are informed by the stories nearest our[6] hearts–whether those stories are found in life experience, family lore, religion, or even in art or fiction. In other words, we believe that our personalities are shaped by the myths we make, and by the archetypes that inhabit them.

Additionally, we found that while the dismal science is often mathematically rigorous, the deeply human instinct to use economics in an *explanatory* way has just as much to do with storytelling as it does with money or math. Whether the question is "what's moving the market," "what does the passage of time do to this security," or "what is a rug-pull,"[7] the economic question of *how* is as much an interrogation of our place in the world as is the question of *why*.[8]

Society has agreed that inedible shiny metals, paper pictures of presidents,[9] and intangible lines of code on the blockchain are all things of value. It's absurd, even farcical. And it's one hell of a mythology. Economics proves, as much as anything else, that just because something is fictitious does not mean it is not real, or not true.

We invite you to consider what stories—whatever shade of fiction they may be—have shaped your personality and your choices. We gen-

---

[4]Look, Mira is a Volatility. It's not her fault she can't do anything halfway.

[5]For once, we are deliberately using "men" to mean "humanity" in this case. We hope the reader sees the joke, and takes it with all the fondness that we intend. See? This isn't an anti-man text at all.

[6]Again, humanity in general. In case that wasn't clear.

[7]And the corollary, "why did no one tell me about this before I put all my money in," to which the answer is *"For fucks' sake!"* We can expand upon this by paraphrasing one of the greatest works of cinema in history: "Memecoins are scams, highness. Anyone who says otherwise is selling one. Never go in against a stranger on the internet when securities fraud is on the line!"

[8]Regrettably, not even Economastrologics can answer the question of *what the fuck*, so we are forced to conclude that this question is impossible to answer.

[9]Or even stranger, royalty. Talk about mythmaking.

tly invite you to examine the gendered way these fictions are handled, in society at large and in your own experience. We believe that fallacy, credulity, and buffoonery transcend gender, as do logic, insight, and intuition; we hope that this silly parody of the little lines that go up and down has supported this argument.

Lastly and most especially, we invite you to indulge your curiosity. We hope the terms we've used and personality traits we've played with have piqued your interest, and we encourage anyone, regardless of gender or background, to get acquainted with investment, trading, *and* astrology.[10] Stay skeptical, think critically, and challenge yourself. There's something to all this mythmaking. You might learn something about the systems around you, or even about yourself.[11]

Besides, navel-gazing as a pastime is about as manly[12] as it gets.

Okay. That's enough of a detour. It's time to get back to what's important, namely, shitposting.

While writing this thousands-of-words shitpost about a six-word meme, we have ascertained a universal truth, which surely should not come as a surprise to anyone who has interacted with a certain type of man: it is far easier to start bullshitting than it is to stop.

Thus, in a feat of self-awareness and self-control that many of our parodied individuals would find truly herculean, we force ourselves to cease babbling and pass the mic.

To the intrepid reader who has made it this far, and who can probably see what's coming: you poor fool. You've been infected with the brainworms, and it's your turn to babble. Let us reiterate the importance of doing so with the confidence and self-assuredness of a mediocre white man.

---

[10] And, we suppose, men. Some of them are worth your time, we promise.

[11] If you've gotten this far and *haven't* learned anything about yourself, you're probably a Fibonacci rising, and we understand you may need some repetition to believe in the unfailing accuracy of Economastrologics. Please go back to Page One and start again.

[12] Whether this implies "men" or "humanity" is a piece of rhetorical irony left to the reader.

Your education in Economastrologics is complete. It is time for you to swagger manfully across the metaphorical stage, receive your pretend diploma, and then *absolutely never shut up* about your MBE.[13] No matter if you're a vegan, play golf, or are a sovereign citizen, these former obsessions matter no more! The first thing you must bring up in any conversation is Economastrologics.[14] Failure to foist this nonsense upon at least five friends, two enemies, and one unwitting male acquaintance will result in seven years of bad luck, regardless of your sign.[15]

Go forth and make sense no more. Or don't. Or do. Whatever.[16] Wield your knowledge to confound everyone in your life. For those on the market,[17] set yourself up for romantic success by pestering all your dates for their signs, risings, and trading strategies.[18]

And now, dear reader, we know your time is valuable. We thank you for wasting some of it on this book. Whatever you choose to do next, whether it is optimizing your trading strategy or throwing the book across the room in annoyance, we ask only that you do it with the same attitude that we brought to this project: wholeheartedly, curiously, and with as much silliness as possible.

Life is too short and too strange to live any other way.

---

[13] A degree in Economastrologics, which is even less useful than a MBA.

[14] Reading this book was a tacit agreement to do so, sort of like how you blindly click "I have read and accept these terms and conditions" for everything.

[15] This callback to early 2000s email chains, MySpace posts, and Facebook copypastas should not be used to judge the authors by age. Judging the authors by their signs or writing skills is not only reasonable, but encouraged.

[16] If you could parse that travesty of mangled grammar, you are even more prepared for your bright future as an Economastrologer than we are.

[17] *rimshot*

[18] We're not going to say "satisfaction guaranteed," not because we are allergic to the word "guarantee," but because that's up to more than just your sign and rising. As it were.

V

ABOUT THE AUTHORS

YLONIA BERGER was the first American to visit the Hanging Gardens of Babylon, or she will be, once she invents a time machine. She loves economics and, begrudgingly, men (especially if they're a Double Top rising—wink, wink). She is a Futures, which was genuinely unplanned and yet hilariously accurate. She is a Fibonacci rising and yes, in fact, is annoyed that Economastrologics actually calls her out. She spends her free time judging everyone and still trying to understand how the male species has survived this long.

MIRA BRAHE is as excellent at being a Volatility as she is at being a Leo, i.e., not very. She was born at exactly 4:00pm, making her both a Double Top rising and Hindenburg rising; to her chagrin, this explains more than it doesn't. She is a direct descendant of famed alchemist and astrologer Tycho Brahe, which gives her an innate understanding of...absolutely nothing, as she made that tidbit up. Some of her best friends are men.

ELVY swore *a lot* when doing these fucking drawings. Normal people ask for portraits of their D&D characters, not made-up shit like crypto. Luckily they are a Volatility with Spread rising, so they have plenty of chaos to make it work. Their interests include books about angry women piloting mechs, movies about vampires, and everything about cults.